What is European

Au cake is the common name for all kinds of cakes originating from the European region. Most European cakes are made from flour and are baked in an oven. Au cake has a characteristic delicious taste, plus a beautiful and eye-catching appearance, so it is increasingly popular with many people.

It is impossible to know exactly when Au cake appeared in Vietnam. From the French colonial period until the American war broke out, Westerners who came and lived in Vietnam made delicious and scrumptious cakes. Before that, Western cakes were also present at trade meetings, important events of the court, and were an important part of parties.

Some famous European cakes in Vietnam such as: regular bread (Lean yeast bread), sweet bread (Rich yeast bread), quick bread (Quick bread), Donuts (donuts), Pancake, Cake / Gato cake, Crepe...

Distinguishing types of European cakes

The common name for cakes with the highest fat content, sweetness for baked goods is cake / gato / .... This is a cake that requires precision in the ratio of ingredients. Simple cake with flour, butter, eggs, milk in Vietnam can be called sponge cake or cake. It will be soft, spongy, full of flavors and shapes.

Cupcake: is a small cake in many ways of cake presentation, usually contained in a pretty paper cup.

Cookies - cookies: The word cookie means small cake. Cookies often use the same ingredients as cakes, but they are smaller in shape and softer, and have a wider variety of flavors.

Chiffon Cakes: Whipping egg whites and yolks separately is the way to soften these cakes. The cake is baked in a tube mold.

Angel food: only use whipped whites, no fat. The cake is light and white as cotton.

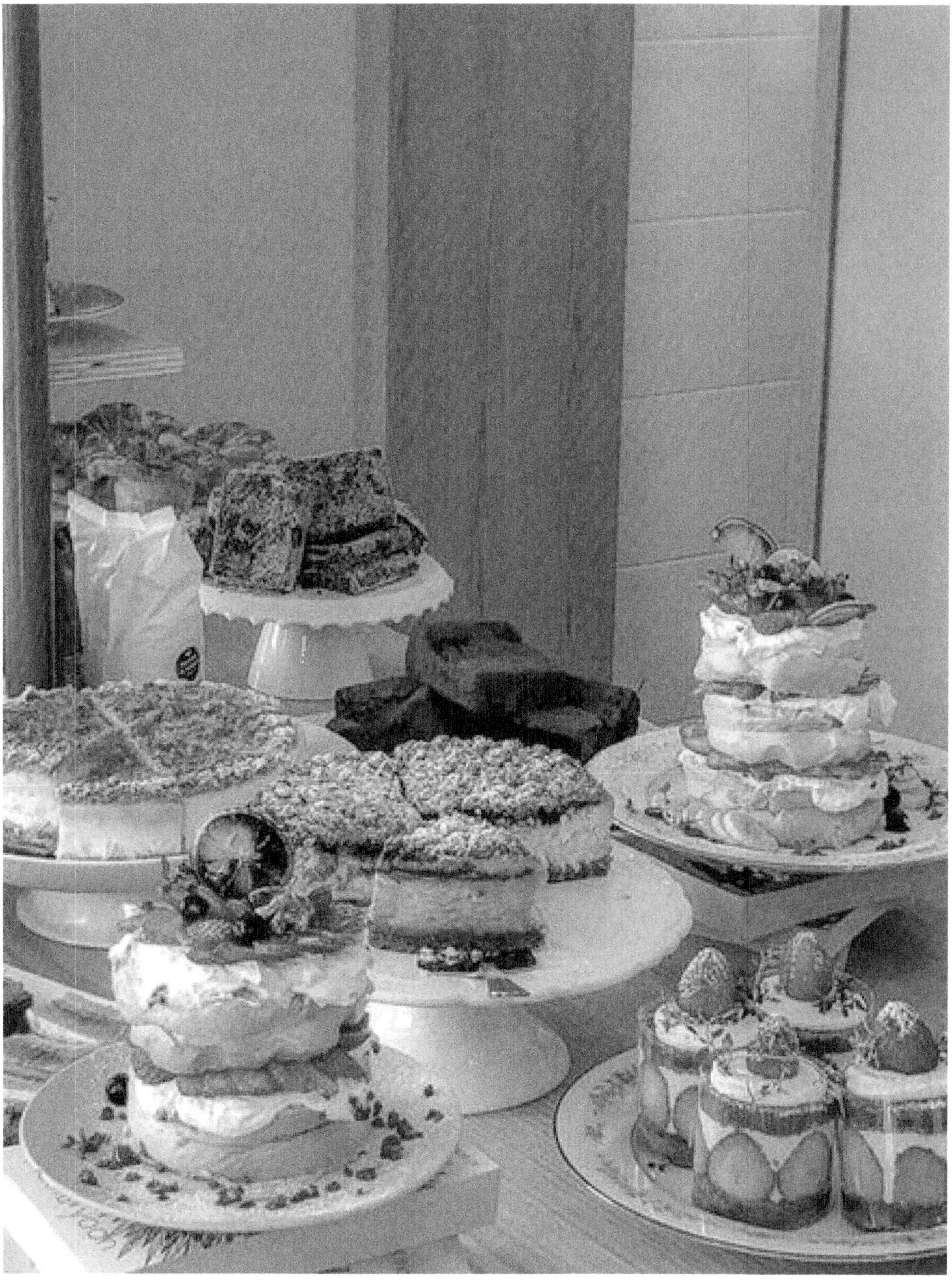

Danisa Cookies

Now you can make them every time you crave them at home with an oil-free fryer. The cakes are made elaborately, fragrant with buttermilk as delicious as the ones in the box, while eating the cake while sipping a little hot tea is really wonderful.

Ingredients for making Danisa cookies with an oil-free fryer

- All-purpose flour 120 gr
- Unsalted Butter 90 gr
- Egg white 1 g
- Powdered sugar 50 gr
- (or fine granulated sugar)
- Raisins 50 gr
- Tools: Air fryer, bowl, spoon, egg beater, ...

How to make Danisa cookies in an oil-free fryer

1. Beat the butter mixture

You put unsalted butter in a bowl, mash it and then add the egg whites and stir well before adding powdered sugar. Whisk the flour mixture until the sugar is completely dissolved.

Tip: You can add 1/2 teaspoon of vanilla and a little salt to the flour mixture, making the cake more flavorful.

2.Mix cookie dough
Sift the prepared flour into the flour mixture, then continue to mix until the dough is smooth.

Tip: The amount of flour should be divided appropriately, avoid adding at the same time because it is easy to make the dough clump and affect the quality of the baked goods.

3. Shape the cake
First, you need to spread parchment paper (or foil) on the griddle of the air fryer. Then, you scoop the flour mixture into the ice cream catcher.

Finally, you shape the cookie on the stencil by drawing a circle with the diameter of the cake.

Tip:
If you don't have an ice cream maker, you can roll the dough, then proceed to cut the slices to taste.
If you want the cookies to look appealing, you can place them in the center of the cake and add raisins, crushed almonds or any other nuts you like before baking.

4.Baking cake
Bake the cake at 140 degrees Celsius for 12 minutes, then use chopsticks to turn the other side of the cake and continue to bake at 160 degrees Celsius for another 5 minutes to complete.

5. Finished product

Cookies made with an air fryer still achieve the crispness and beautiful golden color that is like using the oven! Biscuits are one of the favorite snacks of any age, especially when sipping cookies with hot tea is nothing better.
Tips for making a successful cookie:

The temperature of the air fryer can vary between brands, so use a thermometer to measure the temperature in the pot before baking. This helps the cake to cook evenly and have a nice color. It is possible to separate the right amount of flour when mixing with the butter mixture, avoid adding at the same time because it makes the dough easy to clump, difficult to beat and even affects the quality of the cake.
Separate the egg whites carefully, avoiding the yolks to stick, because it is easy to make the cake taste strange.

Baked Banana Cake

Not only have pure baked banana cake, but now you can make delicious and nutritious baked banana cakes combined with almonds and yogurt in an oil-free fryer that couldn't be simpler.

The cake is not difficult to bake but the result is delicious from the table, the cakes will definitely be a very suitable dessert for you to treat your family after each meal.

Ingredients for making Almond Banana Cake with an oil-free fryer

- Ripe banana 400g
- (about 3 fruits)
- Wheat flour 100 g
- Butter 40 g
- Almond flour 50 g
- Sugar 50 g
- 1 egg
- Vanilla sugar 8 g
- Cinnamon powder 1 teaspoon
- Baking powder 4 g
- Salt 1/4 teaspoon
- Sliced almonds 20 gr

Implementation tools
Oil-free fryer, bowl, mixer

How to make Almond Banana Cake with an oil-free fryer

1. Crush bananas
Peel the banana, then put it in a bowl and mash it with a fork.

Pro tip: If you want to use bananas to decorate the cake, leave about half a banana and slice it into 13 pieces!

2.Mix cake dough
Put in a bowl of bananas 40g melted butter, 1 egg, 50g sugar, 1/4 teaspoon salt, then mix well with a spatula.

Add 1 teaspoon of cinnamon powder, 100g of flour, 4g of baking powder, 20g of almonds, 8g of vanilla sugar and continue to mix.

3. Molding
Brush butter around the sides of the pan, line with parchment paper, then pour in the batter.

Arrange sliced banana on top of cake.

4.Baking almond banana cake in an oil-free fryer
Preheat the air fryer first at 160 degrees Celsius for 10 minutes, then add about 50ml of water and bake the cake for 20 minutes.

After 20 minutes, you lower the baking temperature to 150 degrees Celsius and the last 10 minutes bake at 140 degrees Celsius.

5.Finished product
After the cake is done baking, remember to sprinkle more almonds to make the cake more attractive!

The finished banana cake is fragrant, soft and smooth, with the natural sweetness of ripe bananas and the flesh of crispy almonds.

How to store almond banana cake?
You put the cake in an airtight container or covered with food wrap to avoid drying the cake, store it in the refrigerator and use it for 1-2 days to keep the deliciousness of the cake!

Buttermilk Bread

The sweet smell of buttermilk permeates the kitchen, the beautiful little breads made at home in an oil-free fryer are simple and delicious.

The cake remains soft, chewy and fragrant after baking, the sweet and fatty taste of the typical buttermilk will make you feel hungry just by smelling it.

Ingredients for making Buttermilk Bread with an oil-free fryer

- All-purpose flour 300 gr
- Fresh milk without sugar 60 ml
- Unsalted Butter 50 gr
- Instant yeast 5 gr
- Salt 1/4 teaspoon
- Sugar 2 tablespoons
- 1 chicken egg

Tips for buying ingredients:

Instant yeast, unsalted butter you can easily buy at bakeries selling ingredients or e-commerce sites like Tiki, Lazada, Shopee,... are available.

Implementation tools
Fryer without oil, stencils

How to make Buttermilk Bread with an oil-free fryer

1.Mix cake dough
Put 300g of all-purpose flour and 5g of yeast in a bowl, mix well.

Note about yeast:

Put the salt and yeast at a distance from each other, if the yeast comes into direct contact with the salt, the yeast will die.
Tips to check if yeast is still active or not: If yeast is not stored properly, it may weaken or die, to check if your yeast is still active or not, put it in a cup of warm water. . After about 5 minutes, when you see the enamel bubbling up a lot on the surface of the water, your yeast is still good to use.
Add 1/4 teaspoon of salt, 2 tablespoons of sugar, add 1 egg and 60ml of fresh milk.

Mix well.

2.Kneading the dough
Take the dough out and start kneading the dough. First you fold the dough, then use the back of your hand, press and rub, push the dough away (Folding and Stretching). Note that pressing and spreading the dough away, not down. Rotate the dough 90 degrees, repeat the two steps above.

After kneading for 10-15 minutes, the dough becomes chewy and smooth, add 50g of unsalted butter and dried cranberries and knead in the same way and slowly increase the speed of the dough.

Knead until the butter is incorporated into the dough, the dough becomes soft, chewy, smooth and does not stick to your hands. Break the dough out and pull it into a thin film.

Small tips:

If the dough is a bit dry, you can slowly add a little unsweetened fresh milk!

3.Incubate the dough
Cover the bowl with cling film or a thin cloth and let the dough rise for about 45 minutes, depending on room temperature, for the dough to double in size.

4.Dividing and rolling the dough
Sprinkle a little dry flour on the table, put the kneaded dough with the back of your hand, press and rub, push the dough away (Folding and Stretching). Note that pressing and spreading the dough away, not down. Rotate the dough 90 degrees, repeat the two steps above.

Divide the dough into equal portions according to the size of your pan. Cover the dough and let it rest for about 10 minutes before shaping.

5.Shaping the cake and brewing for the 2nd time
Cakes you can mold into circles, spirals or as long as you like.

Cover the dough and let it rest for about 15 minutes before baking.

Note:

Cover the unrolled dough with a towel or food wrap to prevent the dough from drying out.
Do not be too strong when shaping the cake because it will lose the baking ability of the cake when baking, it will lose its deliciousness.

6. Bake the cake with an oil-free fryer
Line a sheet of foil in the tray of the air fryer, heat the pot at 160 degrees for about 4 minutes

Place the cake in the pan. Bake the cake at about 160 degrees Celsius for 5 minutes, then open the pot, turn the cake and bake for about 5 more minutes until the cake is cooked evenly.

7.Finished product
Buttermilk bread is fragrant, sweet, soft and delicious with a unique buttery smell, isn't it? Let's enjoy now!

Sweet Potato Cake

It sounds strange but delicious is the baked sweet potato cake, more especially, the cake is baked in an oil-free fryer, not an oven as usual! In addition to the traditional baked sweet potato cakes, you can also combine coconut milk or create a beautiful stick shape, making the already delicious cake even more delicious.

Ingredients for making Coconut Milk Sweet Potato Cake

- Sweet potato 180 grams
- Oatmeal 120 grams
- 100 grams peanut butter
- Unsweetened coconut milk 60 ml
- Baking powder 1 teaspoon
- (baking soda)
- Sesame seeds 2 teaspoons
- Tools: air fryer, bowl, spoon,...

Tips for choosing delicious sweet potatoes

Choose potatoes with a round or elongated shape, without waist, hollow, slightly squeezed, not too hard; These tubers are usually low in fiber, high in flour and very sweet to eat.
If you want to buy soft, fragrant, and rotten sweet potatoes, you should choose tubers with a layer of chalk or soil attached to them. When slicing a thin slice at the tip of the potato, you will see a light orange color and melt the sap.

If you want to buy flexible sweet potatoes, you should choose purple-red sweet potatoes with bile stains on the skin. When slicing a thin slice at the tip of the potato, it will be light yellow and plastic.

How to make Coconut Milk Sweet Potato Cake

1.Preparing sweet potato
Put the sweet potatoes in a pot of boiling water (it takes about 15-20 minutes) then take them out and let them cool.

Next, peel off the skin, cut it into circles with a knife, and then crush it with a spoon.

See also: How to boil sweet potatoes in the microwave without water

2.Mix the dough
In turn, put 120g of oatmeal, 180g of mashed sweet potato, 100g of peanut butter, 60ml of coconut milk in a bowl and mix well.

Add 1 teaspoon of baking powder to the mixture and gently mix with your hands until the ingredients are combined to form a smooth dough.

3. Shape the cake
Place the dough on a flat surface, roll the dough into a cylinder, and then use a knife to cut into circles. Use your hands to round and flatten the doughnut shape.

Roll the shaped cake over with a layer of sesame seeds for extra appeal. So the cake shaping is done. Repeat until all ingredients are prepared.

4.Baking cake
Turn on the air fryer 10 minutes before at 160 degrees Celsius to stabilize the heat.

Put the cake in an oil-free fryer and bake at 160 degrees Celsius for about 15 minutes. About 10 minutes turn the cake once so that both sides are cooked evenly.

See more: 9 tips for using an oil-free fryer, housewives need to pay attention

5.Finished product
Coconut milk sweet potato cake after completion will have a light brown color, delicious flesh.

So with just a few steps and simple ingredients, you've got fragrant sweet potato cakes mixed with the fat of coconut milk and roasted sesame.

Cakes can be used for breakfast or snacks. Let's try it now and treat the whole family!

Biscotti

For followers of a "clean" diet, an oil-free fryer is an extremely effective assistant. Now you are no longer sad because the air fryer can help you bake delicious and nutritious biscotti in a snap.

Fragrant Biscotti cake, 1 bite crunchy, sweet taste mixed with crunchy, nutritious nuts, it's worth trying at home.

Ingredients for making Green Tea Biscotti in an oil-free fryer

- Oatmeal 120 gr
- All-purpose flour 80 gr
- Matcha powder 8 gr
- Baking soda 3 gr
- Mixed nuts 80 gr
- 1 chicken egg
- Vanilla essence 1/2 teaspoon
- Honey 30 ml
- Olive oil 20 ml
- Lemon juice 1/2 teaspoon
- Diet sugar 20 gr
- 1 pinch salt

What is Oatmeal? Where do you buy it?

Oatmeal or oatmeal is a food made from oat seeds - a whole grain containing many nutritional values.

To make this powder, people take the oat kernels to separate the shell, then use the method of rolling or grinding them to produce a type of oatmeal that has the same nutritional content as the ingredients used to make it.
You can find oatmeal at grocery stores, supermarkets or online on e-commerce sites.

How to distinguish matcha powder and green tea powder?

Matcha powder is a fine powder made from 100% young buds of the green tea plant. This powder is different from green tea powder in terms of nutritional value as well as price, because green tea powder is only ground from 30% of young tea buds and the rest is 70% of young tea leaves.

Matcha powder has a bright green color and has a bitter after-sweet taste that is different from green tea powder, which is dark green, can be slightly yellow and has a bitter taste.
See details: How to distinguish green tea powder and matcha powder

Implementation tools
Air fryer, egg beater, bowl, spoon, knife, sieve, foil, food wrap,...

How to make Green Tea Biscotti in an oil-free fryer

1. Mix dry mixture

First, you mix 80g of the seed mixture with about 10g of oatmeal.

Tip: This mixing will help the particles adhere to the dough better.

Next, take another bowl and then sift in 110g of oatmeal, 80g of flour, 8g of matcha powder, 3g of baking soda and mix well.

2. Mix wet mixture

Separate the yolks and egg whites into 2 separate bowls.

Then, add a little salt to the egg whites and then use a mixer on low speed until the eggs are foamy like soap.

Next, you add 1/2 teaspoon of lemon juice, 20g of sugar and continue to beat at high speed until the egg is slightly thickened, creating a light peak.

Finally, add to the bowl 1/2 teaspoon of vanilla essence, 1 yolk and then use a mixer on low speed for the mixture to blend.

3. Mix dry and wet mixtures

Slowly pour the dry flour, 20ml olive oil, 30ml honey into the beaten egg and mix until the powder is completely dissolved.

Next, you add the dry seed mixture to the flour bowl and mix again until the mixture is evenly combined.

4. Bake the cake for the 1st time

Preheat the air fryer for 5 minutes at 200 degrees Celsius.

Spread the dough into a rectangle evenly on a sheet of foil with a thickness of about 1cm. Then, you bake this dough for the first time for 15 minutes at 150 degrees Celsius.

After 15 minutes, let the dough cool for about 10 minutes, cover with cling film and place in the refrigerator for at least 3 hours.

5. Bake the cake for the 2nd time

Next, cut the dough into thin slices 1cm thick and then bake for a second time for 5 minutes at 150 degrees Celsius.

Finally, turn the cake over and bake a third time for another 5 minutes at 150 degrees Celsius.

Note: Because the cake has been cut into thin slices, it is necessary to adjust the baking temperature accordingly, to avoid burning the cake.

6. Finished product

Green tea biscotti by air fryer has light green color and attractive aroma. Crispy, sweet and greasy cake from nuts, this is definitely a snack to eat

Whole Wheat Bread

If you are in the process of dieting, try making delicious wholemeal bread from your own air fryer at home. Whole grain bread baked in an oil-free fryer is soft and spongy, chewy, chewy, flavorful, served with delicious fruit jam!

Ingredients for making Whole Wheat Bread with an oil-free fryer

- Whole wheat flour 250 gr
- Instant yeast 3 gr
- Water 170 ml
- Cooking oil 10 ml
- Salt 1/2 teaspoon

Implementation tools
Air fryer, bowl, mixer, round cake mold with diameter 16-18cm,...

How to cook Whole Wheat Bread in an oil-free fryer

1.Mix cake dough
Put in a bowl 250g whole wheat flour, 1/2 teaspoon salt and mix well.

Then, add 3g of instant yeast, 10ml of cooking oil, 110ml of water and continue to mix until the dough is sticky.

2. Kneading the dough

Put the dough on the table and knead according to the Folding and Stretching technique.

First, you fold the dough, then use the back of the table to press and spread the dough away. Note that pressing and spreading the dough away, not down. Next, rotate the dough at an angle of 90 degrees and repeat the two steps above for about 15 minutes.

When the dough becomes a smooth, non-sticky mass, press your fingers to have elasticity.

How to identify satisfactory powder:

The powder is smooth, with good elasticity.
The dough does not stick to your hands: When pressed, it feels a bit sticky, but when you lift your fingers, the dough does not stick to your hands.
The dough can be stretched into a thin film without tearing.
Check the dough with Windowpane. Break off part of the dough, stretch it out. If the powder forms a thin film, it is not easy to tear the light can pass through.

3. Incubate the dough

Place dough in a bowl and cover with cling film for 40 minutes - 2 hours (depending on room temperature) until dough has doubled in size.

Tip to identify the dough: Use your hands to press deeply into the dough, if the dough still has an indentation, it means that it has been brewed.

4. Shape the cake
Knead the dough for 1 minute, roll it up and place it in a baking sheet lined with parchment paper. Cover the mold with cling film and incubate a second time for 40 minutes - 2 hours until the dough has doubled in size.

Use a knife to cut 3 short lines, spread a thin layer of water and then sprinkle black sesame, white sesame on the surface of the cake.

5. Baking cake
Preheat the fryer at 150 degrees Celsius for 5 minutes.

Then, put the cake into the fryer and bake at a temperature of 140 degrees C until the surface is golden brown (time ranges from 20 - 40 minutes depending on the capacity of the fryer).

6. Finished product
Whole grain bread baked in an oil-free fryer is soft and spongy, chewy, chewy, delicious, served with delicious fruit jam!

Crab Bread

To make your breakfast more delicious and full of energy, try making crab bread at home with an air fryer.

The finished crab bread has an eye-catching brown crust, the inside is soft and delicious, the smell of the cake is fragrant and smooth, making everyone in the family love it.

Ingredients for making Crab Bread with an oil-free fryer

- All-purpose flour 250 gr
- Light butter 10 gr
- Yeast 5 gr
- 1 chicken egg
- Sugar 3 tbsp
- Milk 10 ml
- Salt 1 teaspoon

Implementation tools
Fryer without oil, stencils,...

How to make Crab Bread with an oil-free fryer

1.Mix cake dough
You need to put the flour in a bowl and then add 1/4 teaspoon of salt, yeast and mix well.

2.Knead the dough
You continue to add unsalted butter and fresh milk and knead until the dough is soft and smooth.

3.Incubate the dough
Put the flour in a large bowl and let it rest for 30-40 minutes.

4.Kneading and rolling the dough
The flour has risen and risen, knead the dough to remove air and divide the dough into equal parts.

Continue to shape each dough block by rolling the dough into a long cylinder. Note that you roll around so that you can create a large cylindrical block and a small cylindrical block as shown below.

Then you roll out the thin dough to about 0.2 cm.

5.Shaping the cake and brewing for the 2nd time
Use a knife to cut the large end of the rolled dough in half. Fold the 2 ends of the dough just cut out to the sides and slowly roll the whole piece of dough to create a crab bread shape.

Finally, you glue the 2 ends of the dough together to complete the crab bread shape.

After shaping the bread, continue to incubate the crab bread for 30-40 minutes.

6. Bake the cake with an oil-free fryer
Line the bottom of the air fryer with parchment paper and place the cooked crab bread into the pot.

Chicken eggs you put in a bowl, beat well and then use a brush to spread the eggs evenly on the surface of the crab bread so that after baking, the bread has a beautiful color.

You continue to bake the cake with an air fryer for 15 minutes at a temperature of 115 degrees Celsius.

7. Finished product
Crab bread after completion has an eye-catching brown crust, soft and delicious inside. This bread is very suitable for breakfast with your family.

Flan

The flan cake is made by air-frying, after finishing, it is smooth, lightly fragrant with vanilla and has the sweet and fatty taste of custard.

The cake will be more delicious when you eat it with black coffee and shaved ice!

Ingredients for making flan with an oil-free fryer

- Chicken eggs 6 eggs
- Fresh milk with sugar 400 ml
- Condensed milk 120 ml
- Sugar 60 g
- Lemon juice 1 teaspoon
- Vanilla 2 tubes

Implementation tools
Fryer without oil

How to cook flan with an oil-free fryer

1.Cooking Caramel
Put a pan on the stove, add 60g of sugar, a little water, 1 teaspoon of lemon juice.

Stir over low heat until the sugar is completely dissolved. When the sugar starts to boil, shake the pan until the mixture turns brown, then turn off the heat.

Note:

You don't need to add too much water, just wet the sugar. When the caramel is finished cooking, quickly pour a thin layer into each cake mold. Avoid keeping for a long time because caramel is easy to solidify when cooled.

2.Mix egg and milk mixture
Put 3 eggs, 3 egg yolks, 400ml fresh milk, 120ml condensed milk in a bowl, stir in one direction with a spatula to blend.

3.Sieve the milk mixture
Strain the milk mixture through a sieve until smooth.

4.Pour the mold and bake the cake
Preheat the air fryer for 10 minutes at 110 degrees Celsius.

Pour the mixture into each cake mold, then bake for 35 minutes at 110 degrees Celsius.

Finally, put the flan in the refrigerator for at least 4 hours before serving.

\

Note: To know if the cake is done, you can use a toothpick to poke the cake and then pull it out. If the toothpick comes out clean, the cake is done, if the mixture is still sticky, the cake is not done.

5.Finished product
The finished flan is smooth, lightly scented with vanilla and has the sweet and fatty taste of custard. The cake will be more delicious when you eat it with black coffee and shaved ice!
12.Cheese cake

If you are a cake lover, you definitely should not miss the cheese cake made with an extremely convenient air fryer. The cake is soft, fragrant with the smell of cheese, and the light fat thanks to the egg butter is very attractive. With each light touch, the cake is so lovely that you can only look at it but don't want to eat it.

Cheese Cake

Ingredients for making Cheese Cake with an oil-free fryer

- Cream cheese 110 gr
- (cream cheese at room temperature)
- Unsalted Butter 70 gr
- Chicken eggs 4 eggs
- All-purpose flour 100 gr
- Sugar 50 gr

Ingredients for cheese sponge cake in an oil-free fryer

Implementation tools:
Oil-free fryer, bowl,...

How to cook Cheesecake in an oil-free fryer
1. Melt the cheese
Put in a pan 110g cream cheese (cream cheese) at room temperature, 70g unsalted butter.

Turn on the low heat, cook and stir until the mixture melts and blends together, then let the mixture cool completely.

2. Mix cake dough
Separate the whites and yolks of 4 eggs.

Place melted and completely cooled cheese and butter in a large bowl, add 4 egg yolks, and mix well.

Add 100g of all-purpose flour, into the bowl of the mixture above, mix to combine.

3. Whip the egg whites
Place 4 egg whites in a large bowl.

Use an electric mixer to beat on low speed until the eggs are foamy like soap.

When large bubbles appear, add about 20g of sugar, beat on low until the sugar dissolves. After 30 seconds of beating, you add about 20g and continue to beat at slow speed.

When adding the last 10g of sugar to the egg bowl, beat at high speed, beat until the eggs are soft, creamy, the mixture is flexible, glossy and smooth, with soft peaks, then lower the speed for another 1-2 minutes. . Lift down the spire to make it.

Tip: You should divide the sugar into 2-3 parts and then beat in turn with the eggs to dissolve the sugar more evenly.

4.Mix egg whites with cake flour
Add the beaten egg whites in small portions to the flour, stirring gently until all the egg whites are used up.

Mix the ingredients together, so you should mix Fold gently (mixing style and flipping from the bottom of the bowl to the top in one direction) and do not mix too hard to avoid breaking a lot of air bubbles that will not bloom well. Mix only until the flour is evenly incorporated into the egg mixture.

Small tips:

You divide the beaten eggs into small pieces and add several times to make the mixture more even.
Folding the dough will help keep the air bubbles, helping to prevent over-swiping that causes water separation for the eggs. In addition, when mixing the flour, it also helps the dough to be less clumpy, and mixes faster and more evenly. If you want to make cakes that use egg whites to help the cake rise, you need to fold the cake gently.
Tip for those who don't know how to fold, you can use a spatula to gently stir in one direction to reduce air bubbles.

5.Pour the mold and bake the cake
Line the cake pan with non-stick baking paper (you can customize it according to your own mold).

Gently pour the flour mixture into the mold, spreading the dough evenly. Gently pat the bottom of the mold to break up any large air bubbles. Wrap a piece of foil on the face of the mold as shown.

Preheat the oven for 10 minutes before baking to 350 degrees F. Bake at 350 degrees F for 10 minutes and lower to 300 degrees F, bake for another 20 minutes until fully cooked.

6.Finished product
Cheese cake with an oil-free fryer is extremely easy to make but delicious with the fatty flavor of cheese, the soft and fluffy cake layer is so attractive. Let's enjoy now!

Egg Tarts

Ingredients for making egg tarts with an oil-free fryer

- 10 pcs egg tart base
- Chicken eggs 2
- Fresh milk without sugar 150 ml
- Condensed milk 3 tablespoons

How to choose and buy fresh ingredients
How to choose to buy fresh chicken eggs

Eggshell: Should choose eggs with a thin layer of white chalk on the outside, feeling rough or heavy to the touch because these are new eggs. If the eggshell is smooth, bright or has cracks, the eggs are not good for a long time.

Examination: When looking at chicken eggs under the light, if the air chamber is small, the yolk is round, does not move, and the white is transparent with a red orange or light pink color, it is a fresh egg. In contrast, older eggs will be red with many ridges around the cell and large air chamber voids.

Shake gently: Hold the egg to your ear and shake it gently, if there is a sound, it is an old egg, for a long time. If you don't listen, but shake the eggs and see the strong movement, the eggs are broken, the chickens are incubating, ...

See details: How to choose to buy fresh and quality chicken eggs
Where to buy egg tart base?

You can buy egg tart base at baking supply stores, large supermarkets or buy on e-commerce sites. When buying, remember to carefully check the expiration date and packaging of the product to ensure safety!

See also: How to make delicious crispy tart shell at home
Ingredients for egg tarts in an oil-free fryer

Implementation tools
Oil-free fryer, pot, bowl, mixer, sieve,...

How to make Egg tarts with an oil-free fryer
1. Make custard mixture
Put the pot on the stove, add 150ml of unsweetened fresh milk, 3 tablespoons of condensed milk. Stir over medium heat for about 3 minutes until the milk mixture is warm and fuming, then turn off the heat.

Outward remittance:

In order for the milk not to be degraded and lose nutrients, you should not boil the milk, just boil it to a warm level!
For those of you who like to eat sweeter, you can increase the amount of condensed milk depending on your taste.

Beat 2 eggs, then slowly add the eggs to the milk mixture, stirring constantly until well combined.

Next, strain the custard mixture through a sieve to make the tart filling smooth.

2.Make egg tarts
Preheat the air fryer to 200 degrees Celsius for 5 minutes.

Next, place the tart bases inside the pot and bake at 180 degrees C for 4 minutes.

Then, you pour the custard mixture into each tart base and continue to bake for another 7 minutes at 180 degrees Celsius to complete.

Repeat with the rest of the batches until you run out of ingredients.

3.Finished product
Egg tarts are made in an oil-free fryer with a crispy crust, fragrant butter aroma combined with smooth egg cream filling, fatty leopard and moderate sweetness, so eating without feeling bored.

Cat Tongue Cake

Ingredients for Cat Tongue Cake

- All-purpose flour 130 gr
- 100 gr . unsalted butter
- Powdered sugar 110 gr
- Egg white 1 pc
- Vanilla essence 1 ml

Implementation tools
Air fryer, bowl, spoon, stencils, ice cream bag,...

How to make Traditional Cat Tongue Cake

1.Mix butter and sugar
Put in a bowl 100g soft unsalted butter (not melted), 110g powdered sugar. Use a spatula to mix well until combined.

Add about 1ml vanilla, 1 egg white and continue to mix.

Note: You should not add a lot of vanilla because it will make the cake bitter.
Step 1 Mix butter and sugar Traditional cat tongue cakeStep 1 Beat butter and sugar Traditional cat tongue cake
2.Mix cake dough
Divide the dough into 3 parts, add each part in turn to the butter and sugar mixture and mix until the mixture is smooth. Then let the dough rest for 10 minutes.

3.Shaping a cat's tongue
Line a plate with parchment paper and then begin to shape the cake.

Put the flour mixture into the ice cream bag, squeeze the cream into pieces about 3 knuckles long. Remember to leave a little distance, because the cake will expand when it's cooked.

4. Bake the cake with an oil-free fryer
Preheat the air fryer at 180 degrees Celsius for 10 minutes, then bake the cakes at 170 degrees Celsius for 15 minutes.

5.Finished product
Cat tongue cake has a beautiful golden brown color, with a slight smell of butter, when eaten, the cake is crispy with sweet and fatty taste, extremely delicious.

Pumpkin Cake

Pumpkin Cake Ingredients

- Pumpkin 150 gr
- All-purpose flour 250 gr
- Fresh milk 30 ml
- (no sugar)
- Yeast blooms 4 gr
- 1 egg
- Butter 1 tbsp
- Sugar 1 tbsp
- Vanilla extract 1 teaspoon

Implementation tools
Air fryer, bowl, cup, pot, food wrap,...

How to make Pumpkin Cake

1.Steaming and addicted to squash
Peel the pumpkin, then cut it into small pieces. Then steam for about 10 minutes until the squash is cooked.

After the pumpkin is steamed, put it in a bowl and mash it.

Tip for fast and smooth squash mash: Take a strainer to place on a bowl, put the pumpkin on the sieve, and then use a spoon to mash and press down to let the squash pass through the sieve. .

The part of squash that passes through the sieve is small, smooth and even.

2.Mix cake dough
You break 1 egg into the bowl of mashed squash, then mix them well, then add 1 tablespoon of sugar, 30ml of unsweetened fresh milk, 1 tablespoon of butter, 1/3 teaspoon of salt, 1 teaspoon of extract vanilla, continue to mix well again.

Next, you put 4g of yeast in the bowl of pumpkin mixture, mix well. Continue to sift 250g of flour into the bowl of squash mixture.

Finally, you mix everything together and the powder absorbs all the water.

Note: To prevent the dough from clumps, you should divide the flour into several times to sift into the bowl of mashed squash because doing so will absorb the water evenly.

3. Kneading the dough
After the dough has absorbed all the water, use your hands to knead the dough thoroughly until the dough is flexible.

4.Incubate the dough
When the dough is flexible and no longer sticks to the bowl, cover the bowl with cling film and let the dough rest for about 2 minutes.

After 20 minutes of incubating the dough, take the dough out and knead it again for about 1 minute to make it flexible.

5.Shaping the pumpkin
The dough has been incubated for enough time, you divide the dough evenly into 4 small dough blocks. Then roll each dough ball and shape it into a squash shape.

Method 1: Create a shape by cutting a wedge shape

You rub the dry powder into the palm of your hand to prevent sticking, then use your hands to gently press the dough to make it more beautiful.

Rub the tip of the scissors in cooking oil to prevent sticking and make cutting easier, then use scissors to create a petal shape.

Method 2: Column seconds

Use a thin and small string to tie around the dough to divide it into 8 packs as shown.

Note:

Do not tie too tightly because the dough will continue to expand quite large when the second incubation and baking.

6.Baking bread

You use a brush to brush a thin layer of oil on the cakes, so that when baking the cake is more beautiful.

Then, you heat the air fryer for about 5 minutes at 180 degrees. Next, put the shaped pumpkin cake in an oil-free fryer, choose 180 degrees, and bake for about 15 minutes.

After 15 minutes, take out the cake to turn it over and bake it again at 180 degrees for 10 minutes to cook evenly on both sides.

7.Finished product

After baking, pumpkin cake looks like a beautiful yellow-orange pumpkin. The outside crust is crispy, the inside is spongy and soft.

The light pastry taste combined with the fatty taste of butter and milk is extremely delicious and attractive, sure to make my whole family compliment it!

Pumpkin Muffins

Ingredients for making Pumpkin Muffins with an oil-free fryer

- Plain Muffin Remix Cake Flour 250 g
- (or all-purpose flour - flour number 11)
- Eggs 150 g
- (3 fruits)
- Milk 150 g
- Cooking oil 170 g
- Pumpkin 240 g
- (remove shell)
- Raisins and cranberries 50 g

How to choose a delicious pumpkin
Choose pumpkins that are heavy, firm, and have smooth skins. Choose fruit with stalks 2 - 5cm long. Short-stemmed fruits are more susceptible to rapid rotting.
The fruit is round, naturally notched into relatively even parts. Delicious squash is usually yellow-orange, mixed with dark green, yellow in the flesh and has a sweet, aromatic taste and relative plasticity.
See details:

How to choose to buy delicious pumpkin
The effect of pumpkin
How to store pumpkin?
You wash the pumpkin, then put it in a vacuum bag and store it in the refrigerator at a temperature of 5-8 degrees Celsius.

If you want to keep it longer, you should put the squash in the freezer with a temperature of -8 to -10 degrees Celsius. When you want to use it for processing, you should defrost the squash in the refrigerator until thawed, do not thaw with water because water will cause the nutrients of the squash to be washed away.

Implementation tools
Oil-free fryer, bowl, mixer

How to make Pumpkin Muffins in an oil-free fryer

1. Steamed and mashed pumpkin
Steam 240g pumpkin, then mash it with a fork.

Pro tip: You can use a blender to blend the squash to make it smoother.

2. Mix cake dough
Put 3 chicken eggs, 150g milk, 170g cooking oil in a bowl, then mix well to combine.

Next, add 250g of flour and mix until the mixture is light yellow and smooth.

Finally add the pumpkin and mix well.

3. Molding
Pour batter into cupcake pan, sprinkle with raisins and blueberries.

4. Baking cake
Preheat the air fryer at 130 degrees Celsius for 5 minutes, then put the cake in the oven for 22 minutes.

5. Finished product
Pumpkin muffin is extremely fluffy, when you eat it, you can feel the sweet, fatty taste of pumpkin, with the slight sour taste of raisin and blueberry topping. Making this cake to entertain the whole family is a great deal!

Oatmeal Sweet Potato Cake

Ingredients for making Oatmeal Sweet Potato Cake with an oil-free fryer

- Sweet potato 500 gr
- Oatmeal 50 gr
- Condensed milk 2 teaspoons
- 1 chicken egg
- Flaxseed 100 gr
- Fresh milk without sugar 20 ml

Implementation tools:
Oil-free fryer, bowl,...

How to make Oatmeal Sweet Potato Cake with an oil-free fryer

1.Steamed and mashed potatoes
Peel the sweet potato, wash it, and cut it into thin slices as shown. Soak sweet potatoes in diluted salt water for about 15 minutes to remove the plastic, then rinse with cold water.

Prepare a pot of boiling water, put the sweet potatoes in and steam for about 10-15 minutes until completely soft.

Then, bring out the potato puree.

2.Mix cake dough

Put in a bowl of mashed sweet potatoes 2 teaspoons condensed milk, 50 grams of oatmeal, 1/4 cup of flax seeds, 1 egg, and mix well.

If the dough is dry, you can add a little unsweetened fresh milk.

3. Bake the cake in an oil-free fryer
Shape the cake into balls weighing about 40 - 50g.

Put the cake into an oil-free fryer, flatten the cake and fry it without oil for about 2-3 minutes, then turn the surface of the cake until it's cooked.

4.Finished product
Oatmeal sweet potato cake by air fryer is delicious with the natural light sweetness of potatoes, soft and delicious, good for health. Let's enjoy now!

Apple Yogurt Cake

Ingredients for making Apple Yogurt Cake with an oil-free fryer

- Chicken eggs 2
- Sugar 100 gr
- Cooking oil 15 gr
- Plain yogurt 40 gr
- All-purpose flour 100 gr
- 1 apple
- Cream of tarta 1 teaspoon

Implementation tools:
Oil-free fryer, bowl,...

How to make Apple Yogurt Cake with an oil-free fryer

1. Whip the egg whites
Separate egg whites and egg yolks.

Put 2 egg whites in a bowl, add a pinch of salt, add 1 teaspoon of cream of tarta, beat quickly until the eggs are fluffy.

You divide 90g of sugar into equal parts and then add them all in turn, beat the eggs until the sugar dissolves, the eggs are fluffy and have a soft top.

2.Mix cake batter with egg whites
Put in a bowl 2 egg yolks, 10g sugar, 15g cooking oil, 40g pure yogurt, mix well.

Sift into the mixture bowl above 100g of all-purpose flour, mix well to combine.

Add the beaten egg whites in small portions, stirring gently until all the egg whites are used up.

Mix the ingredients together, so you should mix Fold gently (mixing inversion and pushing from the bottom of the bowl to the top in one direction) and not mixing too hard to avoid breaking a lot of air bubbles that will not bloom well. Mix only until the flour is evenly incorporated into the egg mixture.

Small tips:

You divide the beaten eggs into small pieces and add several times to make the mixture more even.
Folding the dough will help keep the air bubbles, helping to prevent over-swiping that causes water separation for the eggs. In addition, when mixing the flour, it also helps the dough to be less clumpy, and mixes faster and more evenly. If you want to make cakes that use egg whites to help the cake rise, you need to fold the cake gently.

3.Cut the apple
Apples are washed, de-stemmed, cut into 8 areca segments as shown.

4.Pour the mold and bake the cake
Line the cake pan with non-stick baking paper (you can customize it according to your own mold).

Gently pour the flour mixture into the mold, spreading the dough evenly. Gently pat the bottom of the mold to break up any large air bubbles.

Arrange 8 apple slices around the cake as shown.

Preheat the air fryer about 10 to 160 degrees before baking. Put the cake tray in, bake the cake for about 20 minutes at 160 degrees C until the cake is completely cooked.

5.Finished product
Apple yogurt sponge cake with a delicious oil-free fryer with delicious apple flavor, strange yogurt taste is really attractive, isn't it? Let's enjoy now!

Fried Milk Cake

Ingredients for making fried milk in an oil-free fryer

- Fried dough 100 g
- Cornstarch 150 g
- Egg yolk 3 pieces
- Fresh milk 110 ml
- Sugar 2 teaspoons

Implementation tools
Oil-free fryer, bowl, mixer

How to make Fried Milk with an oil-free fryer

1. Stir the milk mixture
Put in a bowl 2 egg yolks, 2 teaspoons of sugar, 2 tablespoons of cornstarch. Use a spoon to stir to combine.

Next, you add 110ml of fresh milk and continue to stir.

2. Boil the milk mixture
Put the pot on the stove, add the milk mixture and stir over medium heat until the mixture thickens and thickens.

Coat the mold with a layer of cooking oil and then add the milk mixture. Then put it in the freezer until frozen solid.

3.Cut the milk cake
Cut the cake into small balls.

Coat the milk cake in order: 1 layer of cornstarch, 1 layer of egg, 1 layer of breadcrumbs.

4.Fry cake
Preheat the air fryer to 180 degrees Celsius for 5 minutes.

Line with parchment paper and place the cakes in the pot and fry for the first time for 10 minutes.

After 10 minutes are up, turn the cake over and continue frying at 170 degrees Celsius for another 10 minutes.

5.Finished product
Fried fresh milk cake has a crispy golden crust, the inside is soft, sweet, and full of flavor from milk and eggs.

Bread Roll with Sausage

Ingredients for making sausage rolls with an oil-free fryer

Flour No. 13 100 g
Salt 0.5 g
Sugar 5 g
1 chicken egg
Unsalted Butter 10 g
Sausage 2 pieces

Implementation tools
Oil-free fryer, bowl, mixer

How to cook sausage rolls in an oil-free fryer

1. Mix cake dough
In a bowl, add 100g of flour, 0.5g of salt, 5g of sugar, 1/2 tablespoon of yeast, 1 egg, then mix well.

Note:

Do not allow the salt to ferment directly, as this will cause the yeast to die or become weak. You should mix the flour with salt first and then add the yeast.

During the mixing process, if the dough is not sticky, you can add a little water.

2. Kneading the dough
Knead the dough by hand to form a block, then put the dough on the table and then perform the folding operation according to the Folding and Stretching technique.

First, you fold the dough, then use the back of the table to press and spread the dough away. Note that pressing and spreading the dough away, not down. Next rotate the dough at a 90 degree angle and then repeat the two steps over 10 minutes.

When the dough begins to smooth, add 10g of unsalted butter, then repeat the above kneading for another 10 minutes until the dough forms a uniform, smooth, elastic mass.

How to identify satisfactory powder:

The powder is smooth, with good elasticity.
The dough does not stick to your hands: When pressed, it feels a bit sticky, but when you lift your fingers, the dough does not stick to your hands.
Can stretch the dough into a thin film without tearing
Check the dough with Windowpane. Break off part of the dough, stretch it out. If the powder forms a thin film, it is not easy to tear the light can pass through.

3. Incubate the dough

Cover the bowl of dough with cling film, then let it rest for 45 minutes - 1 hour until the dough has doubled in size.

Small tip: To check if the dough has risen or not, use your hands to press deeply into the dough, if the dough still remains indented, it is good.

4. Shaping sausage rolls

For each sausage, you cut it into 4 parts.

Put the dry dough on the table, knead the dough, then cut it into 5 parts.

Use your hands to roll each piece of dough into a long thread, then place the sausage in and roll the dough.

Cover the dough with a cloth or cling film, let it rest for 30-40 minutes until it has doubled in size.

5. Baking cake

Spread a layer of the egg and butter mixture over the cake.

Preheat the oven to 160 degrees Celsius for 5 minutes, then bake the cake for the first time for 10 minutes.

After 10 minutes are up, turn the cake over and bake a second time for 5 minutes.

pical fleshy taste of sausages. Let's do it and treat the family!

6.Finished product

The batch of sausage bread that has just come out of the oven is fragrant with the smell of butter, when eaten, it has a light sweet and fatty taste with the ty

Raisin Bread

Ingredients for making raisin bread with an oil-free fryer

- All-purpose flour 250 gr
- Fresh milk 100 ml
- (warm up)
- 1 chicken egg
- Unsalted Butter 80 gr
- Sugar 100 gr
- Instant yeast 10 gr
- Raisins 100 gr

Implementation tools:
Oil-free fryer, bowl,...

How to make raisin bread with an oil-free fryer

1.Mix cake dough
Put in a large bowl 250g all-purpose flour, 100g sugar, 10g instant yeast, mix well.

Add 100ml of fresh milk and mix until well combined.

Add 1 egg, mix again.

Tips to check if yeast is still working well: If yeast is not stored properly, it may make it weak or it may die, to check your yeast is still working well or not, you put it in a cup of water. warm.

After about 5 minutes, when you see the enamel bubbling up a lot on the surface of the water, your yeast is still good to use.

2. Kneading the dough
Use your hands to squeeze and mix until the dough is even, into a soft mass, then add 80g of unsalted butter.

Add 100g raisins and mix well.

Knead until the butter is incorporated into the dough, the dough becomes soft, chewy, smooth and does not stick to your hands. Break the dough out and pull it into a thin film.

Small tips:

If the dough is a bit dry, you can slowly add a little unsweetened fresh milk!

3.Incubate the dough
You cover the dough, let it rest for 1-2 hours for the dough to double in size. The dough will rise faster if it is warm and conversely if it is cold the dough will take longer to rise.

4. Roll and shape the cake
After the dough has doubled in size, take it out.

You sprinkle a little flour on the table to prevent sticking, take the dough ball evenly on your hand, fold it, turn it 90 degrees and then fold it again, you do it a few times to make the dough smooth.

Divide the dough into 3 equal parts, then roll the ball into a round shape for the cake.

5.Bake in an oil-free fryer
Preheat the air fryer for about 10 minutes at 160 degrees Celsius.

Put the cake in an oil-free fryer and bake for 20 minutes at 160 degrees Celsius, take out the cake and spray a little water on the surface to prevent the cake from cracking.

Then put the cake in the oven for another 5 minutes at 160 degrees C until the cake is completely cooked.

6.Finished product
Delicious raisin bread with a soft, spongy layer of cake, fragrant with grape flavor and fragrant buttermilk is really attractive, isn't it? Let's enjoy now!

Chocolate Bread

Ingredients for making Chocolate Bread with an oil-free fryer

- Flour No. 13 250 g
- Milk powder 30 g
- Cocoa powder 20g
- Sugar 55 g
- Salt 5 g
- Instant yeast 5 g
- Fresh milk without sugar 215 g
- Unsalted Butter 35 g
- Almond slices 5 gr

Implementation tools
Oil-free fryer, bowl, mixer

How to make Chocolate Bread with an oil-free fryer

1.Mix bread dough
Sift 250g flour, 20g cocoa powder, 30g milk powder into a bowl.

Add 5g of salt, 5g of yeast, 55g of sugar, 200g of unsweetened fresh milk and mix well for the ingredients to blend.

Note: Do not let the salt directly ferment, as this will cause the yeast to die or be weak. You can mix salt and flour first, then add yeast.

2. Kneading the dough

Use the mixer on slow speed for 5-7 minutes for a smooth dough.

When you see a smooth dough, add 35g of unsalted butter to a bowl to soften, then continue to knead at medium speed until the dough forms a ball, does not stick to your hands.

Put the dough on the table and knead it by hand for 2 minutes.

Note:

If you don't have a kneading machine, you can knead it by hand using the Folding and Strectching technique.
First, you fold the dough, then use the back of the table to press and spread the dough away. Note that pressing and spreading the dough away, not down. Next rotate the dough at an angle of 90 degrees and then repeat the two steps above for 15-20 minutes.
How to identify satisfactory powder:

The powder is smooth, with good elasticity.
The dough does not stick to your hands: When pressed, it feels a bit sticky, but when you lift your fingers, the dough does not stick to your hands.
The dough can be stretched into a thin film without tearing.

Check the dough with Windowpane. Break off part of the dough, stretch it out. If the powder forms a thin film, it is not easy to tear the light can pass through.

3.Incubate the dough
Put the dough in a bowl, cover with a towel and let it rest for 45 minutes - 1 hour until the dough has doubled in size.

Small tip: To check if the dough has risen well, use your hands to press deeply into the dough, if the dough still remains indented, it is good.

4. Roll the dough and shape the cake
Knead the dough for 1 minute, then divide it into 9 parts, each about 65g and then roll.

Line the mold with parchment paper, put the dough in and rest for the second time about 30 minutes - 1 hour for the dough to double.

5.Baking bread
Preheat the air fryer to 180 degrees Celsius for 5 minutes.

Brush fresh milk on the bread, sprinkle more almond slices and bake at 180 degrees C for 18 - 20 minutes.

6.Finished product

Chocolate bread is soft and elastic, each cake is chewy, sweet and sweet, with a unique aroma from cocoa powder, extremely attractive.

Tips for successful implementation

If you do not use instant dry yeast, you must activate the yeast with warm water or milk at 35-40 degrees Celsius, stir well and let it rest for 5-10 minutes until the yeast blooms to form a crab-like patch. Do not get hotter because it will kill the yeast or weaken its activity.)

If using instant yeast, you should use instant yellow yeast for high-fat and high-sugar breads.

Do not put salt and yeast directly together, it will make the yeast weak and can kill the yeast.

If the dough does not rise after incubation: Please check the expiration date of the yeast, if the yeast is close to the date, the ability of the yeast to function is weak and the yeast may die. To test, you can mix a little warm water about 30 degrees (not more than 37 degrees). Put the yeast in and wait for about 15 minutes, if the enamel is bubbling like a layer of crab bricks, the glaze is still good, you can rest assured to use it.

Should knead the right technique so that the dough forms a gluten bond, when the bread is finished baking, the new bread will be soft.

Tips for preserving cakes

Store bread in an airtight container/bag, in a cool place. Can be used for 2-3 days.

Keto Bread

Ingredients for making Keto Bread with an oil-free fryer

- Coconut flour 75 gr
- Almond powder 55 gr
- 7 chicken eggs
- Unsalted Butter 60 g
- Vanilla 1 teaspoon
- Baking soda 1 teaspoon
- Cream Cheese 60 ml
- Baking powder 1 teaspoon
- Cinnamon powder 1 teaspoon

Implementation tools:
Oil-free fryer, bowl,...

How to make Keto Bread with an oil-free fryer

1.Mix all cake ingredients
Heat butter and cream cheese by microwave or water bath.

In a blender, combine melted butter and cream cheese, 5 eggs, 75g coconut flour, 55g almond flour, 1 teaspoon cinnamon powder, 1 teaspoon vanilla extract, 1 teaspoon baking soda, 1 teaspoon of baking powder.

Finally, add 2 eggs to the blender.

Blend the flour mixture evenly.

Small tips:

You can use chopsticks or a flat spatula to gently stir the flour so that the blender will not weigh the machine. You should mix for about 1 minute and then let the machine rest for 1-2 minutes and then grind again, avoiding the machine from burning.

2. Molding
Line the pan with parchment paper or spread a layer of butter to prevent sticking. Pour the dough into the pan and spread the cake evenly.

3. Baking bread
Put the dough tray into the oven and bake in an air fryer at 120 degrees for about 45 minutes until the cake is completely cooked.

4. Finished product
Simple but delicious air fryer keto bread with delicious coconut, almond flavor and good for health. Enjoy this delicious cake now!

Apple Bread

Ingredients for Apple Bread

- Wheat flour number 13 300 gr
- Sugar 50 gr
- Instant yeast 4 gr
- Fresh milk 180 ml
- Unsalted Butter 25 gr
- 1 chicken egg
- 1 apple

Implementation tools:
Oil-free fryer, bowl,...

How to make Apple Bread

1.Mix bread dough
In a large bowl, add 300 grams of flour 13, 25 grams of sugar, 4 grams of instant yeast, 1 egg and mix well.

Add 180ml of fresh milk and mix until well combined.

Tips to check if yeast is still working well: If yeast is not stored properly, it may make it weak or it may die, to check your yeast is still working well or not, you put it in a cup of water. warm.

 After about 5 minutes, when you see the enamel bubbling up a lot on the surface of the water, your yeast is still good to use.

2. Knead the bread dough

Use your hands to squeeze and mix until the dough is even, forming a flexible mass, then add 20g of unsalted butter.

Knead until the butter is incorporated into the dough, the dough becomes soft, chewy, smooth and does not stick to your hands. Break the dough out and pull it into a thin film.

Small tips:

If the dough is a bit dry, you can slowly add a little unsweetened fresh milk!

3. Incubate the dough

Cover the dough, let it rest for about 1 hour, until the dough doubles in size. The dough will rise faster if it is warm and conversely if it is cold the dough will take longer to rise.

4. Apple slug

Peel apples, remove seeds. Then cut the pomegranate as shown.

Put the pan on the stove, turn on medium heat, when the pan is hot, add the remaining 5g of butter, add 25g of sugar, stir until the sugar is melted.

.

Add the chopped apples and stir well, cook over medium heat until the apple juice thickens, the apples are clear. Let the filling cool completely.

5. Shape the cake

After the dough has doubled in size, take it out.

You sprinkle a little flour on the table to prevent sticking, take the dough ball evenly on your hand, fold it, turn it 90 degrees and then fold it again, you do it a few times to make the dough smooth.

Divide the dough into 4 equal parts. Then roll out the dough, put a little apple filling on top, wrap the dough tightly and round the cake.

Place the cake into a cupcake pan lined with parchment paper. Stick up a small tree branch for decoration.

6. Baking cake

Preheat the air fryer for about 10 minutes at 175 degrees Celsius.

Put the cake in an air fryer and bake for 15 minutes at 175 degrees C until the cake is completely cooked.

7.Finished product

Apple bread by air fryer is extremely delicious with a golden crust, delicious sponge bread with sweet and delicious apple filling. Let's enjoy now!

Tips for successful implementation:

After use, yeast should be put in a sealed glass or plastic container and stored in the refrigerator to avoid opening the lid often. Yeast is good to use within 6 months and do not use expired yeast to make cakes.

Uneaten cakes can be wrapped, kept in an airtight container or ziplock bag for 1 week, stored in the freezer for 1 month, when eaten, defrost in the refrigerator and then put in the microwave for a little while. Re-warm, the cake will be delicious, not dry. You should make the cake according to the correct ratio to make the cake delicious.

Almond Cheese Cookies

Ingredients for making Almond Cheese Cookies in an oil-free fryer

- All-purpose flour 50 gr
- Almond flour 50 gr
- Cheese powder 30 gr
- (Japanese Wakodo powder)
- Powdered sugar 40 gr
- Unsalted butter 60 gr
- 2 egg yolks
- Vanilla essence 1/2 teaspoon
- Cooking oil 1 teaspoon

Implementation tools
Air fryer, egg beater, round mold diameter 7cm

How to make Almond Cheese Cookies in an oil-free fryer

1. Puree butter and sugar

Put in a bowl of 60g unsalted butter, 40g finely sifted powdered sugar, and beat with an electric mixer at medium speed until the butter turns light yellow.

Next, add 1 egg yolk, 1/2 teaspoon vanilla essence and mix well to combine.

2. Mix cake dough

Put in a new bowl 50g flour, 50g almond flour, 30g cheese powder and mix well.

Then, sift the flour mixture into the butter bowl and use the mixer on low speed until just combined.

Use your hands to knead the dough to form a ball.

3. Rolling the dough

Put the dough in between 2 layers of wax paper, then use a rolling pin and put it in the refrigerator for 30 minutes to harden the dough.

4. Shaping and baking

Preheat the air fryer for 15 minutes at 130 degrees Celsius.

Use a round mold to press on the dough to cut the cake.

Stir in 1 egg yolk with 1 teaspoon of oil. Gently brush the mixture over the top of the cake and then use a pointed fork to draw wavy lines.

Put the cake in an air fryer and bake at 130 degrees C for 8-10 minutes.

Pro tip: If you use an oven, set the temperature to 170 degrees Celsius and bake for 8-10 minutes.

5.Finished product

Cheese crackers just came out of the oven smells delicious, the cake is crispy until it's soft, melts in the mouth, sweet, fatty, fleshy, extremely attractive.

25.Salted Egg Sponge Cake

Ingredients for making salted egg sponge cake in an oil-free fryer

Salted Egg Sponge Cake

Ingredients for salted egg sponge cake in an oil-free fryer

- Flour No. 8 40 gr
- Fresh milk without sugar 36 gr
- Salted eggs 3
- Egg yolk 6 pieces
- Cooking oil 136 ml
- Sugar 65 gr
- Orange juice 10 gr
- Lemon juice 3 gr
- Vanilla essence 2 gr
- Salt 1/3 teaspoon
- Rub cotton a little

Implementation tools
Air fryer, egg beater, mixer

How to cook salted egg sponge cake in an oil-free fryer

1.Mix the cake flour mixture
Put in a bowl 4 egg yolks, 36g fresh milk, 36ml cooking oil, 40g finely sifted flour, 1 finely sifted salted egg, 2g vanilla essence. Use a whisk to stir the mixture until combined.

2. Whip the egg whites
In a large bowl, add 4 egg whites, 3g lemon juice, and beat with an electric mixer on low speed until the eggs are foamy like soap.

Divide 45g of sugar into 3 parts, add each part and beat until dissolved. Beat each sugar for about 30 seconds on low speed, then add the next sugar to beat.

When adding the last part of sugar to the eggs, turn on the mixer at high speed, beat the eggs until the eggs are stiff, creamy, the mixture is flexible, glossy and smooth, lift the spatula to create a vertical tip.

Note: Egg whites should be at room temperature before whipping.

3.Mix cake batter with egg whites
Divide the beaten egg whites into three parts. First, you put a part of whipped cream into the cake mixture, then use a whisk to gently stir all ingredients together.

Put the mixture just stirred into the bowl of egg whites and then use a spatula to gently mix the mixture from bottom to top. Bring the spatula to the bottom of the bowl, lift the heavy ingredients, and fold aside. Continue until the mixture becomes smooth.

4.Pour the mold and bake the cake
Preheat the air fryer to 115 degrees Celsius for 15 minutes.

Line with parchment paper and pour the dough into the mold, bake at 115 degrees Celsius for 60 minutes.

5.Make egg oil sauce
Put in a bowl 1 egg yolk, 10g orange juice, 20g sugar, 1/3 teaspoon salt and stir well.

Then, slowly add 100ml of cooking oil to the bowl, stirring while stirring until the mixture is thick, thick and light yellow.

6.Finish the cake
Spread the egg oil sauce evenly on the cake, cover with cotton balls, and puree salted eggs to finish.

7.Finished product
Soft and sweet sponge cake blended with greasy egg oil sauce, salty and extremely delicious.

Purple Sweet Potato Bread

Ingredients for Purple Sweet Potato Bread

- All-purpose flour 350 gr
- Purple sweet potato 400 gr
- Fresh milk 90 ml
- 1 egg yolk
- Salt 1 teaspoon
- Sugar 150 gr
- Unsalted butter 30 gr
- Instant yeast 5 gr
- Material figure
- Ingredients for purple sweet potato bread

Implementation tools
Oil-free fryer, non-stick pan, ...

How to make Purple Sweet Potato Bread

1.Mix bread dough
You put 300g of flour, 1 teaspoon of salt, 50g of sugar and 5g of yeast in a bowl and mix well.

Then you add fresh milk and egg yolks into the flour mixture.

Note: Yeast and salt should be placed far away from each other, do not pour directly on each other. Salt will weaken the activity of yeast when in direct contact with each other.

2. Kneading the dough
Use your hands to knead the dough until it is sticky. Then start stuffing by Folding and Structching technique.

First, you fold the dough, then use the back of your hand to press and spread the dough away. Note that pressing and spreading the dough away, not down. Next rotate the dough at a 90 degree angle and then repeat the two steps over 10 minutes.

When the dough begins to smooth, add 30g of unsalted butter, then repeat the above kneading for another 15 minutes until the dough forms a uniform, smooth, elastic mass.

How to identify satisfactory powder:
The powder is smooth, with good elasticity.
The dough does not stick to your hands: When pressed, it feels a bit sticky, but when you lift your fingers, the dough does not stick to your hands.

The dough can be stretched into a thin film without tearing. Check the dough with Windowpane. Break off part of the dough, stretch it out. If the powder forms a thin film, it is not easy to tear the light can pass through.

3.Incubate the dough
Place the dough in a bowl, cover with cling film and let rise for about 60 minutes until the dough has doubled in size.

Tip: You can check if the dough is well-rested by pressing deeply into the dough with your hand. If the indentation stays the same, it is OK.

4.Make purple sweet potato filling
Purple potatoes are washed and cooked in a steamer, then pureed sweet potatoes with a blender.

Next, put the mashed potatoes in a non-stick pan, along with 50 grams of sugar and 20 grams of flour, put on the stove and proceed to slug at medium heat.

You keep slurping until the potatoes are flexible and become a non-stick mass, then turn off the stove.

5. Roll the dough and shape the cake
After 1 hour, the dough has risen, then you bring the dough out and knead it again and divide the dough into 4-5 small parts.

You flatten the thin dough and put the sweet potato filling in the middle and then roll it into a ball. You roll the cake with the long filling, then use the tip of the knife to cut the middle of the upper layer of dough, finally roll the cake.

6.Baking cake
Brush a thin layer of egg onto the cake before baking. Turn on the air fryer at 170 degrees Celsius before 10 minutes. Finally, you put the cake in the oven for 15 minutes at 170 degrees Celsius, then flip the side and bake for another 5 minutes at 170 degrees Celsius, then the cake is cooked.

7.Finished product
So there was immediately a bread filled with purple sweet potato that was very soft and flexible, the more I liked it, the more I liked it, but it didn't cause boredom.

Cheese Seafood Pizza

Ingredients for Cheese Seafood Pizza

- Pizza base 1 pc
- Black tiger shrimp 300 gr
- Squid squid 200 gr
- 2 bell peppers
- Purple onion 1 piece
- Butter 1 tbsp
- Mozzarella Cheese 100 gr
- Ketchup 1 tbsp

Implementation tools
Oven or fryer without oil, knife, pan, stove,...

How to cook Cheese Seafood Pizza

1.Preparing and marinating seafood
Shrimp you peel off the shell, remove all the head and tail, use a knife to make a slit on the back of the shrimp to easily remove all the shrimp.

Buy squid to peel off the outer skin, wash and cut into circles.

Add in the shrimp and squid 1/2 teaspoon salt, 1/2 teaspoon sugar, 1/2 teaspoon pepper and 1 teaspoon seasoning. Mix well and let sit for about 10 minutes.

Tips for preliminarily cleaning shrimp and removing the back of shrimp quickly

Method 1: Peel the head and shell of the shrimp body from the foot, to the tail, use two fingers to hold the end part and then pull it out. Next, use a knife to cut the shrimp's back to reveal the black thread and then take out a toothpick.

Method 2: After the shrimp have been washed, insert a toothpick in the middle of the shrimp's neck, then pull out the black thread and remove it.

Method 3: Wash the shrimp, use scissors to cut along the shrimp shell to reveal the black thread, then wash it under running water to clean.
Tips for preparing clean, non-fishy ink

Cut across the body and remove any viscera remaining inside the squid body. Use a knife to lightly cut a line on the outside of the head of the squid body to peel off the skin of the squid. Rinse with white wine, ginger, vinegar or lemon to completely remove the fishy smell.

2.Preparing other ingredients
Buy bell peppers, wash, cut into small squares about 1-2 fingers. Sliced purple onion in circles. Thinly slice chili, remove all seeds.

3. Stir-fry seafood
Put on the stove 1 pan, wait until hot, saute onion and minced garlic. Put all the seafood in and stir-fry on high heat until you can turn off the stove.

4.Pour the filling on the cake base
Spread a layer of ketchup evenly on the pizza base, arrange all the red onions, bell peppers, and cheese on top of the cake.

Add seafood and a few slices of chili on top and prepare to grill, can add another layer of cheese on top if you like.

5.Baking cake
Method 1: Bake pizza in the oven

First, you need to open the oven first to preheat it, open it at 200 degrees Celsius for 10-15 minutes. When there is enough time, put the cake into the oven at 230 degrees Celsius for about 7 minutes.

Method 2: Bake pizza in an oil-free fryer

For an air fryer, preheat the oven for 5 minutes at 180 degrees, then bake the pizza at 200 degrees for 10 minutes.

6.Finished product

The hot, crispy pizza comes out of the oven with seafood mixed in a layer of greasy cheese served with bell peppers, making it even more attractive.

Save the recipe now and go to the kitchen to show off your talents for the whole family to enjoy!

Salty Tarts

Ingredients for making Salty Tarts with an oil-free fryer

- 5 tart base
- Minced pork 100 gr
- Liver pate 80 gr
- Onion 1/2
- (diced)
- Seasoning 1 little chili powder 1 little
- (salt/pepper)
- 1 piece mozzarella cheese

See also: How to make a tart shell

Ingredients for savory tarts in an oil-free fryer

Implementation tools
Air fryer, egg beater, mixer

How to make Salty Tarts with an oil-free fryer

1. Marinate meat
Put in the meat bowl 1/2 diced onion, 80g liver pate, a little salt, pepper and paprika and mix well.

2.Baking the crust
Preheat the air fryer to 180 degrees for 15 minutes.

Use a fork to pierce the cake base and bake at 180 degrees for 5 minutes.

3. Bake the cake for the 2nd time

Put the filling in the middle of the cake and bake it a second time at 150 degrees for 10 minutes until the cake is cooked.

When the filling is done, cover with a little mozzarella cheese and bake for the last time for 5 minutes at 180 degrees Celsius.

4. Finished product

When you try a piece of tart, you will feel the crunchy, fluffy crust blended with rich, fatty cheese from cheese, extremely delicious.

Garlic Butter Cheese Bread

Ingredients for making Garlic Butter Cheese Bread with an oil-free fryer

- Flour No. 11 270 g
- Flour No. 8 60 g
- Sugar 55 g
- 2 eggs
- Salt 10 g
- Fresh milk 140 g
- Yeast 4 g
- Unsalted Butter 40 g
- Whipping cream 70 g
- Lemon juice 1 tablespoon
- Unsalted Butter 150 g
- Minced garlic 60 g
- Condensed milk 50 g
- Honey 2 tablespoons
- Dried parsley 2 tbsp
- (dried parsley)

Tools: air fryer, bowl, spoon,...

Parsley, also known as dried parsley, is a very commonly used spice in cooking. You can buy them in big supermarkets, European spice shops or bakeries selling ingredients.

How to make Garlic Butter Cheese Bread with an oil-free fryer

1.Mix the dough
You put 270g of flour number 11, 60g of flour of number 8, 35g of sugar, 1 egg, 2g of salt, 140g of fresh milk, 4g of yeast in a large glass bowl.

2.Stuff the dough
Then use a mixer to beat the dough in one direction at the lowest level (if you don't have a dough mixer, mix the ingredients well and then put it on any clean surface and knead for 5-7 minutes) until the bread dough is smooth, Non-stick hand is satisfactory.

When the dough is smooth, add 40 grams of unsalted butter and continue kneading for about 5 more minutes until you try to pull the dough and the dough is supple.

You roll the dough into a glass, wooden or plastic bowl, cover with cling film, and rest for about 1 hour until the dough has doubled in size.

Pay attention when fermenting using iron, metal will easily damage the enamel, you should use wooden, glass or porcelain, porcelain bowls to ferment.

3. Make cream cheese mixture

You put 200 cream cheese, 70g whipping cream, 20g sugar, 1 tablespoon lemon juice in a bowl and use a whisk to beat for about 5 minutes until the mixture is smooth and smooth (if you don't have a whisk, you can use a whisk to beat it)..

Put the mixture in an ice cream bag and put it in the fridge.

4. Make Garlic Sauce

You put 150g of melted unsalted butter, 60g of minced garlic, 50g of condensed milk, 1 egg, 2 tablespoons of honey, 2 tablespoons of dried parsley (dried parsley) in a bowl and mix well, then add cool refrigerator compartment.

5. Divide and knead the dough

After enough time to rest the dough, at this time, the bread dough will double in size. You continue to put the dough on a flat surface and knead the second time for about 1 minute to break the air bubbles, then divide the dough into 6 equal parts and shape into round cake blocks.

Cover 6 parts of dough with cling film and let rest for another 60 minutes. After baking, the bread dough will expand.

6. Baking cake

You preheat the oven to 170 degrees Celsius with Pre-heat mode and press start / start to make the temperature in the fryer more stable.

Line a layer of parchment paper in the cake tray, put the cake in an oil-free fryer and bake at 165 degrees Celsius for 10 minutes.

When enough time is up, take the cake out and cut the cake into 6 (leaving the bottom of the cake uncut).

Remember to let it cool down a bit before cutting it, because when it's hot, it will break easily.

7. Fever pump

You take out the cream sauce and pump it evenly on 6 sides of the bread, then brush a layer of garlic butter sauce on the surface of the cake (if you like to eat a lot of sauce, you can dip the bread side into the sauce bowl).

8. Bake the cake for the 2nd time

You put the bread into the tray of the air fryer, inject a layer of cream sauce on the surface of the cake, and bake the second time at 160 degrees Celsius for 10 minutes.

If you want to eat crispy bread, you can adjust the baking temperature at 180 degrees Celsius for 7 minutes.

9. Finished product

When the cake is cooked, take it out on a plate and enjoy. This garlic butter cheese bread is fragrant, fatty, cheese, buttery, crispy on the outside and soft inside, suitable for snacking or for breakfast with fresh milk is also very delicious and attractive.

Basic Sponge Cake

The soft, fragrant and fluffy sponge cake made from an oil-free fryer still retains the same deliciousness and sponginess as when the water is in the oven. In addition to eating the cake, you can add cream, fruit, sauces, ice cream to serve or make a beautiful birthday cake to give to your friends and relatives.

Ingredients for making 3-flavoured mini sponge cake in an oil-free fryer

- Chicken eggs 2
- Wheat flour 30 gr
- Milo powder 1 teaspoon
- Matcha powder 1 teaspoon
- Vanilla 1/2 tube
- 1 handful of raisins
- Lemon juice 1 tbsp
- Sugar 1 tbsp
- Salt 1/2 teaspoon
- 1 little cooking oil

How to choose to buy fresh chicken eggs

When choosing to buy chicken eggs, you should observe the color of the eggshell, so choose those with dark skin, without tiny black spots on the surface of the shell.

Fresh chicken eggs normally the surface of the eggs will be slightly rough, when gently shaken, you will not hear the egg moving.

On the contrary, do not choose eggs with pale color, smooth egg surface, when shaking, you can hear the sound of eggs moving inside because these are eggs that have been stored for a long time and may have been damaged.

See details: How to choose to buy fresh and quality chicken eggs Ingredients for 3-flavoured mini sponge cake in an oil-free fryer

Implementation tools
Oil-free fryer, mini cake mold, cage stirrer, spoon, sieve, bowl, flat spatula,...

How to cook 3 flavors mini sponge cake with air fryer

1. Beat egg yolks and whites
Using 2 eggs, separate the yolk and white into 2 different bowls. With the egg whites, use a hand whisk to beat the egg whites until large bubbles appear. Then add 1 tablespoon of lemon juice and continue to beat with a spatula for 1 minute.

Next, add 1 tablespoon of sugar. Beat the whites and sugar continuously for about 10-15 minutes, then add the rest of the sugar. Continue whisking until the whisk is lifted and the whites form a vertical peak.

Gently stir the egg yolks. Strain the egg yolks through a sieve to make the cake mixture smoother.

Next, sift 30g of flour and 1/2 teaspoon of salt into the bowl of egg yolks, stir until the yolks and flour blend together to form a smooth paste.

2.Make a cake

Scoop 1/3 of the beaten egg whites into the bowl of yolks, gently stir from the bottom up to combine the 2 mixtures.

Next, add this mixture to the egg whites. Stir well and gently to form a smooth paste. At this step, be careful not to stir vigorously to avoid bursting air bubbles.

Divide the cake mix into 3 equal parts, the first bowl will add 1/2 vanilla bean, the next 1 teaspoon milo powder, and the last bowl 1 teaspoon green tea powder. Use a spatula to gently mix these 3 mixtures.

3.Baking cake

Prepare the cake mold, spread a little oil inside the mold. If you have stencils or cupcake molds to line them with, there's no need to grease them.

In turn, pour the flour mixture into each cake mold, decorate with some raisins (or nuts, dried jam depending on your preference) on top.

Note: Only fill the mold about 1/2 full so that the cake has space to expand when baking!

Preheat the air fryer for 10 minutes at 150 degrees Celsius. Then place the cake molds in the pot one by one, bake the cakes at 130 degrees Celsius for 15 minutes.
After baking for enough time, check that the cake is done by inserting a toothpick into the cake, if the mixture does not stick to the toothpick, then the cake is done.

4.Finished product
Mini cake with 3 flavors in an oil-free fryer with 3 irresistible delicious flavors, made quickly.
The cake is soft, moist and fragrant with vanilla, milo and matcha, guaranteed to satisfy the taste of each family member.

Taiwan Pineapple Cake

The Taiwanese pineapple cakes baked in an oil-free fryer have an eye-catching golden brown color, the crust is soft and sweet, the pineapple inside is soft, sweet, sour, and extremely delicious. You don't have to look any further, because now you can make them at home surprisingly quickly and simply.

Ingredients for making Pineapple Cake with an oil-free fryer

- Pineapple 1 fruit
- Sugar 30 g
- All-purpose flour 150 g
- Unsalted Butter 120 g
- Egg yolk 1 pc
- Condensed milk 35 g

How to choose delicious pineapple

Color: you should choose the fruit with bright yellow color from the stem to the tail, there will be a few green eyes but it still has a certain sweetness.
Shape: Round, short pineapples will have more flesh than long ones.
Pineapple eyes: Choose the fruits with large, sparse pineapple eyes because this shows that the pineapple is old and ripe naturally, not soaked in medicine.
Fragrance: you can try to smell it at the end of the fruit, if it smells good, you should buy it.

In addition, you should not choose fruits with a slightly sour smell in the way of fermentation, because the pineapple is overripe.
Pineapple top: The greener the pineapple top, the fresher the pineapple. Overripe pineapples will have dry or brown tops.
Hand feel: Delicious, fresh pineapple will not be too hard nor too soft, when pressed with your finger, there will be no feeling of indentation.

Implementation tools
Oil-free fryer, bowl, mixer

How to make Pineapple Cake with an oil-free fryer

1.Preparing pineapple
Peel the pineapple, wash it, remove the core, then cut it into small pieces.

Quick pineapple cutting tips:
First you cut the two ends of the pineapple, then stand the pineapple upright and peel it from the top down.
Next, cut in half, make a V-shaped cut to remove the hard core in the middle of the pineapple.

2. Pineapple jam slug
Puree the pineapple, then put it in a non-stick pan with 30g of sugar over low heat.

When the pineapple filling is combined into a thick, flexible mass, the pan is dry.

3.Mix cake dough
Put in a bowl 120g unsalted butter, 35g condensed milk, 1 egg yolk and stir with a spoon.

Next, finely sift 150g of flour into the above mixture, then mix well for the mixture to blend, forming a mass.

Cover the dough with cling film and place in the refrigerator for 40 minutes.

4.Shaping pineapple cake
Divide the dough and multiply into 10 equal parts and roll into balls.

Flatten the dough, put the filling in the middle and then round it.

Cover the mold with a little dry flour, put the cake in and then press to shape, use a razor to cut a few more lines to create more textures.

5.Bake in an oil-free fryer
Preheat the air fryer to 180 degrees Celsius for 10 minutes.

Brush a thin layer of egg on the cake, then put it in the oven for 10 minutes at 160 degrees Celsius.
After 10 minutes, flip the cake over and bake for another 10 minutes.

6.Finished product
Pineapple cake has an eye-catching golden-brown color, the crust is soft and sweet, the pineapple inside is soft, sweet, sour, very delicious

Pineapple Sponge Cake

Besides the usual sponge cake, you can combine with fragrant, sweet and sour pineapple and then bake it in an extremely convenient oil-free fryer. The beautiful golden pineapple cake, spongy and fragrant with a very strange pineapple scent, is very suitable for you to show off your talents in those family parties.

Ingredients for Pineapple Cake

- Pineapple 1 fruit
- Butter 120 gr
- Sugar 170 gr
- 2 eggs
- Wheat flour 200 gr
- Cornstarch 20 gr
- Fresh milk 125 ml
- Cream tartar powder 1/2 tbsp

Tips to choose good pineapple

Color: Choose pineapples with an even yellow color. If the pineapple is too green, the pineapple is not ripe, the sweetness will not be high.
Shape: Choosing round, short pineapples will be more fleshy than oblong ones.
Feel with your hands: Use your hands to gently press the pineapple body, choosing pineapples that are not too soft or too hard.

Pineapple eyes: Choose to buy fruits with large and sparse pineapple eyes, which proves that the pineapple is ripe naturally, not soaked in medicine.

Fragrance: Choose pineapples that are fragrant, do not choose pineapples that are unripe because they are unripe or have a slightly sour smell in a fermented way because these are overripe pineapples.

Pineapple tops: Choose pineapples with fresh green tops, do not choose fruits with dry, wilted, brown tops.

Implementation tools
Air fryer, knife, pot, cup

How to make Pineapple Cake

1.Preparing pineapple

Pineapple cut off the top of the pineapple and peel it around. After peeling, you skillfully use a knife to remove the pineapple eyes and cut into thin circles, removing the middle core.

2.Cooking caramel

Put a pan on the stove, add 60g of sugar, a little water, 1 teaspoon of lemon juice.

Stir over low heat until the sugar is completely dissolved. When the sugar starts to boil, shake the pan until the mixture turns brown, then turn off the heat. Pour caramel into each mold.

3.Mix the egg yolk mixture
Eggs separate yolks and whites. Put in a bowl 2 egg yolks, 120g butter, 20g cornstarch, 200g flour, 125ml fresh milk and 50g sugar and mix well.

4. Whip the egg whites
The egg whites are put in a bowl with 35g of sugar, then beat with a mixer at low speed, lightly beat by hand.

When you see the mixture is milky white, smooth, thick, lift the whisk to see that the eggs form a standing top, turn the bowl upside down to see that the eggs do not fall.

5.Mix cake batter with egg whites
Next, add the yolk mixture earlier into the white mixture and fold gently and evenly.

6.Pour the mold and bake the cake
Arrange pineapple in each fragrant layer in the mold and then pour in the caramel layer. Then pour the cake mixture on top.

Preheat the air fryer to 125 degrees for 5 minutes.

Then bake the cake 3 times, the first time at 140 degrees Celsius for the first 20 minutes, the second time at 150 degrees Celsius for 15 minutes and the last time at 160 degrees Celsius for 10 minutes.

7.Finished product
So there is a delicious pineapple cake right away, the golden color of pineapple with sweet and sour taste, so attractive, isn't it?

Contents

- Danisa Cookies — 5
- Baked Banana Cake — 9
- Buttermilk Bread — 13
- Sweet Potato Cake — 19
- Biscotti — 24
- Whole Wheat Bread — 29
- Crab Bread — 33
- Flan — 37
- Cheese Cake — 39
- Egg Tarts — 41
- Cat Tongue Cake — 46
- Pumpkin Cake — 53
- Pumpkin Muffins — 58
- Oatmeal Sweet Potato Cake — 62
- Apple Yogurt Cake — 65
- Fried Milk Cake — 69
- Bread Roll with Sausage — 72
- Raisin Bread — 77
- Chocolate Bread — 81
- Keto Bread — 86
- Apple Bread — 89

- Almond Cheese Cookies — 94
- Salted Egg Sponge Cake — 98
- Purple Sweet Potato Bread — 102
- Cheese Seafood Pizza — 107
- Salty Tarts — 112
- Garlic Butter Cheese Bread — 115
- Basic Sponge Cake — 120
- Taiwan Pineapple Cake — 125
- Pineapple Sponge Cake — 130

Printed in Great Britain
by Amazon